Contentions with Joy

a poetry collection

Donella McLean

TRANSCENDENT ZERO PRESS

HOUSTON, TEXAS

PUBLISHED BY TRANSCENDENT ZERO PRESS
www.transcendentzeropress.org

ISBN-13: 978-1-946460-15-8
Library of Congress Control Number: 2019941961

Printed in the United States of America

Transcendent Zero Press
16429 El Camino Real Apt. #7
Houston, TX 77062

Cover artwork: Faith Cherry, "Rays of Hope"
Cover Design: Glynn Monroe Irby

FIRST EDITION

Contentions with Joy

a poetry collection

Donella McLean

Acknowledgements

To my brother, James Dornwell and Heather Dornwell and their family, I give thanks for always supporting me. To Faith Cherry, I want to thank you for the use of "Rays of Hope," and for always being there for me. To Dustin Pickering, for re-typing all my poems…thank you. To Transcendent Zero Press for continuing to partner with me…I appreciate all the great work you do. Above all, I thank God for being my Creator and Father, the Author of my life.

To Mareena, A wealth of joy be with you always.

Contents

A Letter to Joy

Dear Joy,

Fate has let You escape me
She has exchanged day for endless night and
sleep for insomnia.
She has made the
darkness of yesterdays into
my hallowed home.

Make that night null!
Relinquish her grasp on
my withering flowers of
funeral wishes.

Make her black frantic dances into
slow skin to skin waltzes, filled with
Your enlightened splendor.

Let her labored breath fall into steady
and rhythmic hushes.

Help me, Joy! I need to break
from those stifling hugs of
sorrow and make them kisses
of happy plum lipstick and
green buds that blossom into
life anew.

With utmost sincerity,

Donella M. McLean

The Elusive Happiness

The elusive happiness,
a triumph to achieve, a
celebratory glee.

I'd give anything to grasp it
and hold it and dwell deep
in it "Give me a chance!"
I pray, to claim happiness for
more than a day.

I've lived with much distress
and my life's been a mess but
The elusive happiness deserves
a loyal friend like me, the
kind that endures and never
leaves.

I'd make an excellent companion to
happiness, if she'd let me.

Ardella Darling

Your life was hard, coarse, and chaotic… You
lost shrimp boat captain daddy at fifteen, the
boat stands still then sways away. At twenty,
your fireman lover joined the army leaving
you in pieces and pregnant

Della dearest,

Later, you found an affinity for Nicky at a mental health clinic
he became your husband and ex five times thereafter all told
you had two boys and two girls all of whom you loved and left,
You couldn't locate an elixir for the mania and depression,
The clash of moods.

Della damn it!

You strove to concoct a perfect dosage
of the mellowing meds just to sustain
your kids but horse tranquilizers were
too much, even for you,

Mommy dear,

At fifty you were put in a nursing home
couldn't walk, couldn't breathe
You were left ruminating the past.
as you retired in solitude with
only the occasional visit,
you were left to
Lick your wounds.

Sunday Glory

White and violet blossoms
Phonographs in shape,
Triumphs of nature can
only bloom so long, a
short window in the
life of a flower. Their
clinging vines grabbing
the hands of a metal fence,
Trumpeting to church goers
"It's Sunday morning!"

We don our dressy attire and
gather our bibles awaiting the
heavenly message only to become
distraught when church is over
and the morning glories are gone
in the brilliant blaze of spring sun.

Paper Boy

Fall over backwards.
Fall over forwards.
Fall over as
You move toward her.

Calmly and slightly
Yet oh how quietly
She moves to embrace
With courage and grace.

Hardly even noticed
You see her treachery.
All the same,
As you fill with shame.

Calmly and slightly
Yet oh how swiftly
She moves away,
Away from her prey.

Tears of sorrow
Tears of pain
Tears of what was
Once an obvious gain.

What she wanted,
You could not give.
The way she wanted,
You could not live.

Fall over backwards.
Fall over forwards,
Fall over it as
If it were normal.

Drowning

The past security
Has suddenly turned to hatred
And as I face your criticism
I find nothing constructive.

The guiding light you used to carry
Is now dead and gone
And I no longer wish to follow
In your footsteps.

And your once soothing character
Has turned to hostile greed
And I won't be here to watch
You drown in your own blood.

Dreams of Murder

I stand immobile,
Numb, and torn –
From your abuses.
The tormenting words
Spat in my face
Cling silently and
The self-evident
Hatred in your beadlike
Eyes have demolished
My intended life.
And the passion
That surges through
My veins is thicker
Than any blood and
Stronger than my soul –
But the immoral
Thought of killing is
Keeping me sane –
        SOMEHOW
Only in my dreams
Can I escape your
Torture, only in
My dreams do I
Cause Your pain.

Singing Lessons

Music began with a box fan, the
eighties in Florence, Texas, a sultry
and sweaty summer like emerging
from a bath wet moisture sticks a
little too long. My siblings and I
would sing songs into the humming fan
morphing our noise
to an elevated gospel.

Then three girls at thirteen sang hymns
like "Canaan Land is Just in Sight"
into a microphone at church, budding
belief like sweet flowers, a not so
classic melody.
Who knew then what we would become?

But the saddest day came when while
riding and singing in his old Ford
midnight blue truck Daddy said
"You can't carry a tune!"

Throwing Away a Cake

The gaudy perception of
chocolate unfettered frosting on
a decadent cake, a supplant of
birthday wishes six months
past my birthday's gone.

Waddle through another day
yellow mix of a way with
crimson raspberry filling
succumbing to well churned cravings
eating a slice of it then
throwing the rest away.

A wasteful act that's necessary for
a new diet.
It's burning down the house to
get rid of those pesky roaches.

Women at Twenty
After the poems by Donald Justice and Maurya Simon

Women at twenty,
Learn to speak fearlessly
Through their hollow halls,
Trying to fill them.

Dancing in merriment,
They feel like
Under them life is an elevator,
Shifting up and down.

Deep in dormitories
They unearth
Sexuality's blooming flower-beds,
How it opens them.

And in that youthful bed,
Wrinkles have yet to gather.
They are more and more free now.
Something is covering them, something

That is like the warm blanket
Of self-love's magic, weighty,
Concealing immaturity's constant pain
Behind pretty
lipstick laughter.

Women at Twenty *Revisited*
After the poems by Donald Justice and Maurya Simon

Women at twenty
Shed shyness's clinging
Coat for brave flirtation
With lusty experience.

Dancing in merriment,
They waltz with fun
As it leads them step by step to
Freedom from mother's molds.

They unearth blossoms
Of self-definition
And begin to shape the petals
Of future purpose.

With painted faces,
At the height of shine
They don veneers of pretty clothes
In a hue of vanity.

They are mannequins of
Immaturity hiding
The haunts of adolescent pain
Behind the defense of pretense.

Antiquated or not I found
you when radios were still
worth listening to… a
modicum of my being came
through the airwaves that
winter, the morsel that
attracted you for a
millisecond then evaporated
like water on a chilled
Windowpane.

Between the Noise

Static radio noise mixed
in its you between the
fuzz and how I feel
for you…breaking through and,

Clinging to the station for
some clarity now
it's like a piece of hard candy
stuck to my desk…
You ring true, you are the

music through the static,
the best song ever heard
melody beseeches the
static to relent.

Static cling will see us through the
noise, noise, fuzz, fuzz that
debilitates the music…that's what
I feel…I'm captivated by your
breath on my skin…the static…in
the air…you the music in between
All the noise, noise, buzz, fuzzing

it's way to my ear…the breath
hot, radiating.
that's why I listen to
the static station, I'm

listening for you to Sing
my soul a new tune.

In a Warehouse, Without a Name

The Latin we know,
The Latin we speak
The nights we spoke volumes to each other.

But this was the most I could handle…thus far at
Sans Nomen Services (SANS for short).

An exercise in limitless work, an
activity I could aspire to…
warehouse wonders,
boxes bantering from slide to truck

These were involuntary movements, involuntary
emotions like rapturous ardor
        Moving down the slide
into his lap–lost in explanation

Christmas season delivering and loading boxes
led me to wanton wanderings with an
unattainable man– above me, beside me,
around me
        Made me more
Made me work arduously.

For he is *sans nomen*
and *sans* love, mostly
sans hate…for me Now
we are *sans* night

Unrequited Love

Unrequited love:
unconsummated intentions
enraptured bliss and torment
simultaneously.

Scrumptious offerings leaves the
tongue longing for a nibble, the
decadent, luscious pastry you can't
even savor.
It's window shopping for the
tongue…the flavor you've
been craving.

It's tension in the seams
of a pair of tight jeans…
continuous contention.
Strangled by the emotion,
demoted to voyeur.

Guessing at Normal

Choosing a time to stand my ground
But once again I back down
             I'm guessing at normal.

Wanting them to see the sunny side
Not the black gloomy tide
             I'm guessing at normal.

"You'll never please them all."
But hell, I sure have tried
             I'm guessing at normal.

My hypothesis isn't correct
The test is too difficult
             But that's *guessing* at normal.

I want to fit in
But the clothes weren't made for me.

Guessing at normal
Guessing at right
Guessing at happy
Guessing at life

Klimt's Kiss

Two blooming loves

His lips tackling
the hunger pangs
of this Kiss
Like no other abandon
seeping into
               this lurid cliff

She clings onto the
transcendence of their
flower Witnesses
framing this escape
waking the subtleties
Once golden dawn breaks

How too can we Embrace?

When will I be good enough?

You think I'm mundane,
simplified equation, all
insignificant
masquerade elation.

You scan my pretense,
give me another name,
"Quirky, crazy" lady. I'll
use you just the same

Grab a hold of me!
squeeze out that easy stuff.
Marinate me, Master!
Make me more than enough.

Email me some day.
that letter wasn't read:
I'm irrational now, Who
should I be instead?

Match with Me

This is a boxing match
between me and me.
The me: diseased, infected
And me: living, corrected

With the gloves of candy-colored
pharmaceuticals, attractive to the eye
but swallowing them is…
Round one: night and day,
Round two: day and night,
Round three: and again (gets so tedious).
And the rounds go on.

With the simultaneous fight of
me-moods and me-thoughts
Which will concede defeat?
Give me one more round!

In a boxing ring with gloved-
me and deluded-me who's
more likely to upper cut those
prescription drugs?
In a Southpaw's manner,

It's a technical knockout!

Hard Lessons Learned

My "Marriage" – an
experience (enough)
an insight into
suppression.

But the clenching "crush"
Let me breathe
again.

I was freed,
made whole… slowly
becoming,
with the potent swaying wind,

The one who would transcend
tomorrow's sadness and
emerge into
today's more suited
         Dance…
              Happy, happy…
                  Dance.

Cancerous

Conjugal touches
with acid hands
seeping into
my core, eroding
those poison lies of
I love you's.
Eat my nerve endings
crumbling the vows
that the priest blessed into
frothing fizz,
left with fickle, untamed emotion.

I'm scarcely even
here now,
now that the acid's been
puked up,
poured out over
our "marriage."

I'm dissolved
like sugar in hot tea
What was the affect?
A new mixture.

In contrast–

He's left me
with light, airy
free caresses
of conversation
(not so intimate)
But significant salient,
striking words that I
love to recall and
transform into
I love you truths, those
words I've learned
to live by.

I've sown
them into
my head,
letting their
tendrils braid
into my gray matter,

They are kisses of
remission.

Metamorphosis

Caterpillars invading me,
eating these emotional
processes… they writhe in well-fed
ecstasy, sure that I'm the one to be
tasted, this time.

Wallowing into the pores of my
skin… little by little tattooing their
poison deeper to the root of the
matter, while twisting those needle
teeth…

They can't get enough!

I taste *that* rich to these
sweet-toothed devils of
destruction….

And then they're stagnant in
a stoic cocoon,

Opening in 10 long years
into the butterfly whispers
of that new escape!

My Version of Pandora's Box

I'm on assignment
closing him in a
box, to forget him
to get that closure
from his heavy stuff

Those cardboard blankets covering
this *him*
and me I became real,
in his presence
another new life…

Opened fissures of
untamed honesty
so heady it's been
evaporating
yesterdays into

rich, oblivion, residual
trash, store in my attic
tape them up-flaps:
excess motion

crawl space in my head
can't let me escape,
version twenty-five let
evil illness out, but not
all hope.

For Lisa

Reminiscent of
Manor Road house
where she made a
strawberry cake
with pale pink icing.

So kind her Life
did shine.

Like pretty treats of
blankets and bottles and
her precious baby girl,
who made her world.

It's too short,
It's a complete dessert,
Tastes sweet.

Her one last bite concludes with
the tender yet sudden
cessation… that cold winter's
end.

To My Daughter, Mareena Katheleya McLean

Her presence my message
an eternity in one face
grown from love into an
adult who's cherished and
adored.

Pressed into my arms the
totality of her being a hug of
her knowledge intelligence
beyond her years.

I'm filled with tears as I recall
her first cry, the moment she
made herself known and
whether happy or sad I'm
beside her either way.

Along the way youth sheds
yet we're like sisters but
more than friends she'll
always have my hand.

A present she's always been every
year she keeps giving that
supreme presence, her
cheerful essence her
glowing smile carrying her
into twilight and
tomorrows.

–I love you always, your mama

Divorce: The Desertion

Now that I'm deserted,
abandoned by my "spouse,"

Now I'm divorced, torn shunned,

Now I'm tainted.
I'll even admit that I'd loved
him once when "we" were
new…

Now I'm forsaken, discarded
and wanted,
rejected and ruined

Now that I'm frozen in fear,
exposed to the world,
This snow and avalanche,

Now in the elements,
barren, those chances are
gone and the wound
isn't so fresh, I'm awake
and surviving this frost
bite despite this
nakedness, broken and
alone, this amputated
kind of surface me, no
more to be seen, covered
in cold waiting for a coat
of a cure, an end to sad.

Now that our vows have been
shattered, a piece of ice
crystal shards, on my own,
longing for a love, but how
could someone want me?

Donella Says

Donella says
"I'm done with Arturo!"

He didn't know
her anyway...

Just how she felt
at night
lying in the same

loveless slumber

Donella goes
alone now...

manages smiles even.

But no more kisses... no
more pretense.

Now middle age
has crept onto
this pyramid of
soft flesh.

And the haplessness
of being single keeps
her sorry and sane
now...
        Somehow.

Suggested by the song "Jane Says" by Jane's Addiction

Awestruck in Transit

Obscured view
of a truck hauling a covered trailer
from a car window driving along
the freeway, 'I wonder what it
contains," I say.

Then out -pops- a horse's head
Neighing like the devil,
Desperate for release

Then out -pops- a second horse's head
Licking the air for moisture,
Heat radiating… it's crowded in there.

Then out -pops- a third horse's head
Waving from inside side to side then
Nodding in agreement that the air
Flowing past him feels splendid

The horses are wonder enough

But the guard is out and on the prowl
I see him as I pass the trailer…
A cattle dog… eyeing an auspicious visitor…
Approaching the bed of the truck, I glide on
by in awe.

I Came, I Fell, I Got Up Again and Again

I can't say, "I came, I saw, I conquered"
because I haven't conquered anything and
I've done more than just see life happen.

I've fallen and been forgotten more times than
I can count and I've managed each time to get
up but the trial still lingers on.

I'm not well-spoken but I've been somewhat
well-written, the story endures it seems.
Life has been the Instigator. And yes, the
defendant is guilty as charged.

The duration of the sentence remains to
be seen but something tells me I'm in for
a few more falls, a lot more charges.

Lackluster future and demented past, plan
for the taking… wait for the verdict.
I've come to expect that all but forgotten falls
will happen. They keep me occupied.

Sure-footed to a fault… I'd like to be.
Instead I'm unsteady and waiting for
the Instigator to trip me up.

The inevitable happens it seems.
It's easy to forget the tormented.
Unless you're the one always suffering.

Life in the Periphery

Life as a peripheral person is
lonely. Just observing on the
sidelines, unseen– mostly, but
more than that– unnoticed.
Life in the periphery.

In some other world and
dimension– withdrawn.
Foreboding future lies ahead.
The only escape from
Life in the periphery

is to move into full view.
No more hiding, denying
life for what it is,
emphatically social
friends, family– the norm.

And not so much periphery.

Respite from the Sun

Catch a glimpse of
blackbird pecking at
water from a drip,
drip, drip– ping hose.
Caught in

heliolatry, he
basks in the
sunlight, thirsty
and wanting like
a yearning new-
lywed ready to
don her new
trousseau: shiny,
invigorat-
ing clothes. He skips

skips, skips like a
rock on a water down
the swelter- ing
cemented porch,
still jostled by the
water, this onyx
feathered creature
getting ready to flit
away–he's quenched
anew. "Now fly!"

My Journey with Joy

My relationship with joy has always been
an elusive one. When she's eluding me
hides in the shadows and doesn't show
her face.

When she's open to view she gathers
around me like feathers… wrapping me in
joy's softness, the tender happiness
penetrating the sadness crashing like waves
arriving on shore.

When she's being elusive she's under the radar
creeping in for the occasional subtle joke.
She needs the attention, but it comes slowly.
My life has been in contention with happiness;
A contention that sweeps up the joy.

Give Me a Fourth Focal

I'm surrounded by that "fourth
focal"– point to worse than
bi- or tri- focals, it's less to be
seen.

Give me vision for another day,
the kind of seeing that's
satiation when you're starved
for sight

It's the remedy to the
blight of blindness,
the calculated cure.

It's the kind that takes away the
blurring hummingbirds, those
depths of disillusioned lenses.

Of the Sea

To Mareena, which means "of the sea."

Lunar precision
Mother of the waves guides
them home honing her
babies into repetitive
motion making
moments crash
forward onward forward

The waves are like traffic
intermittent pile ups
careening onto shore.
Moon mother says, "of the sea"
I say, "part of me" dancing the
sway it seems crashing waltzes
in the sand.

Spoonful of Sea

I'm more of a spoon
girl than fork
Spoon me a bit of the sea, like
a pelican taking a big gulp a
portion of evaporated water
will suffice, leave me a salty
mess

Concentrated, the breeze
sea air flowing swiftly
ripened on shore making
odor of air.

Mix Tape Biographical Sonnet (Donella Marie Dornwell McLean)

"How You've Grown" by 10,000 Maniacs
"Dancing with Myself" by Billy Idol
"The Boy with the Thorn in His Side" by The Smiths
"Half a Person" by The Smiths
"Interesting Drug" by Morrissey
"Joey" by Concrete Blonde
"Cool Scene" by Dandy Warhols
"Pancho and Lefty" by Willie Nelson

"Crazy for You" by Madonna
"Closedown" by The Cure
"Shake the Disease" by Depeche Mode
"I Will Survive" by Cake
"Colorblind" by Counting Crows
"Love" by The Sundays

"Clocks" by Coldplay
"Here's Where the Story Ends" by The Sundays

Humanity's Insatiable Desire for More

The more I know about
Wanting more, the less
I want to know.

Why must we always crave more?
It baffles me that people are insatiable.
High standards aside, give me a break.
I need to be content in my own shoes.
Grant me some peace because
Wanting more is exhausting and grating.

Grate me some more.
No, I take that back.

I'm
Finished
I
Want
Nothing More.

Contentions with Joy

A masquerade of me
dragged down and
weighing heavy
no remedy in sight
a need for more clarity

tugging me down
tendrils tangled up
the sadness revealed
the contention is real
Wake up, fight back,
don't let it
Drown you, look to

Joy... the kind I've
dreamed of
the kind that exists in
golden sunshine
Rays of happiness they
exude the life
I want.
escape the sadness and
deliver me
back to Joy, a mother I
always needed.

Honey Dose

So when I tell my friend she needs
Her honey dose of Prozac…
The dose that lasts for years and keeps
You stable for a long while.
Not forever because that kind of dose
Doesn't exist. But every so often
A honey dose takes hold and keeps
You going… it's what you wish for on
Psychiatric meds. Too bad doctors
Think changing your meds is preferable.
I think they are unhinged. Things can go
Well for a while in the house of the mentally ill.
Give me something sweet to take my mind off of it.
A reprieve from mini meltdowns.
Here's to the honey!

Just Some Word Milk

Like a cow
Coming home to graze
In a well learned pasture
Not so green, just yellow-gray
They line me up to dine
In a mental hospital
Cattle prod me some more
Keep me in line
Scan me with a metal detector
Because I'm a danger to myself–
Not others–
Big cow full of word milk
Scans the dining room for a seat
Isolated in the pasture of tables
A mixture of patients and plows of plans
The same mix of cows and monstrous medications
Not people and problems
Keep me contained
Like a carton of milk

A Summer in Austin

The nights at SANS
were summer filled
heat clouded air
becoming stagnant and
full of humidity.
The air was so full
there wasn't room
for me.
I was crowded in the
corner of a SANS truck,
breathing was labored
The air crushed me
I was squelched in
the aftermath
of sunny humidity
each night.
He played me heavy
melodies in the midst of
heated mental fissures.
Too bad we weren't
meant to be.. I'm
still struggling with
my steamy hot sanity.

Kaleidoscope of Thoughts

Kaleidoscope of thoughts
interweaving into one another
a dreamscape while awake
filtered through gray matter
brewed to my brain
trying to find order
in this disorder of a stream
river flowing roughly
rush me closer to shore
a bed full of wrinkled linen
needing to be made
make me a new scene
mountainous mental energy
ephemerally it fades
to the next thought and thought
and thought.

Slow universe like him
Devours brilliant voice
Always wild open prisoner
Born broken embrace poetry
Picture concrete red color
Bleeding belly hard desire

Linger cake of joy
Blue sky
Essential warmth
Whisper laughter
Beneath a cloud of
Ocean breeze

Happy bluebird in spring
Dare to sing
Smile song for your soul
Breath will always hope
Wish your dream before you follow through
Each wonder warm and true

Velvet peace
Dancing about
Which world is this
Listen like magic
Melt by rain
Ferocious life candy

Trust sunshine
Tiny star life
Almost shine
Comfort like barefoot
In tickle-ly grass
This is happiness

BIOGRAPHY

Donella McLean is originally from Central Texas and now lives there again. She won the Quill and Scroll Award in high school. She has had her poetry published in the Austin International Poetry Festival anthologies. Other poetry collections by Ms. McLean include *Answer to My Ellipsis* and *I've Come Unstirred*.

www.ingramcontent.com/pod-product-compliance
Lightning Source LLC
Chambersburg PA
CBHW031614040426
42452CB00006B/520